COLLECTIVE

Contents

Original Artwork by Todd Murphy
Photography: Clay McBride
Art Direction: Larry Freemantle

Transcribed by Kenn Chipkin & Matt Scharfglass
Project Manager: Aaron Stang
Book Layout: Odalis Soto

WARNER BROS. PUBLICATIONS - THE GLOBAL LEADER IN PRINT
USA: 15800 NW 48th Avenue, Miami, FL 33014

WARNER/CHAPPELL MUSIC
CANADA: 85 SCARSDALE ROAD, SUITE 101
DON MILLS, ONTARIO, M3B 2R2
SCANDINAVIA: P.O. BOX 533, VCNDEVAGEN 85 B
S-182 15, DANDERYD, SWEDEN
AUSTRALIA: P.O. BOX 353
3 TALAVERA ROAD, NORTH RYDE N.S.W. 2113

Carisch
NUOVA CARISCH
ITALY: VIA M.F. QUINTILIANO 40
20138 MILANO
SPAIN: MAGALLANES, 25
28015 MADRID

IMP
INTERNATIONAL MUSIC PUBLICATIONS LIMITED
ENGLAND: SOUTHEND ROAD,
WOODFORD GREEN, ESSEX IG8 8HN
FRANCE: 25 RUE DE HAUTEVILLE, 75010 PARIS
GERMANY: MARSTALLSTR. 8, D-80539 MUNCHEN
DENMARK: DANMUSIK, VOGNMAGERGADE 7
DK 1120 KOBENHAVNK

SHANE EVANS
Drums

DEAN ROLAND
Rhythm Guitar

WILL TURPIN
Bass

ED ROLAND
Lead Vocals, Guitar

ROSS CHILDRESS
Lead Guitar

PRECIOUS DECLARATION

Words and Music by
ED ROLAND

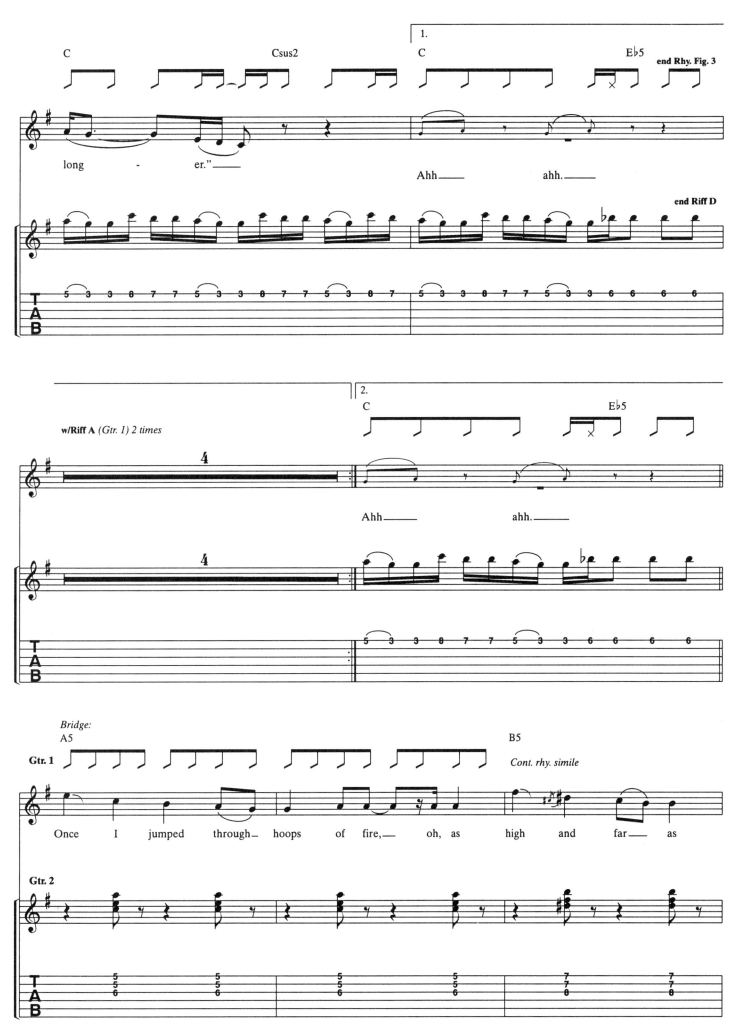

Verse 2:
New meanings to the words I feed upon
Wake within my veins
Elements of freedom.

Pre-Chorus 2:
Whoo, can't break now,
Yeah, I've been living for this.
Whoo, won't break now.
I'm cleansed with hopefulness.
(To Chorus:)

LISTEN

Words and Music by
ED ROLAND

Listen - 5 - 1
0028B

Pre-Chorus:

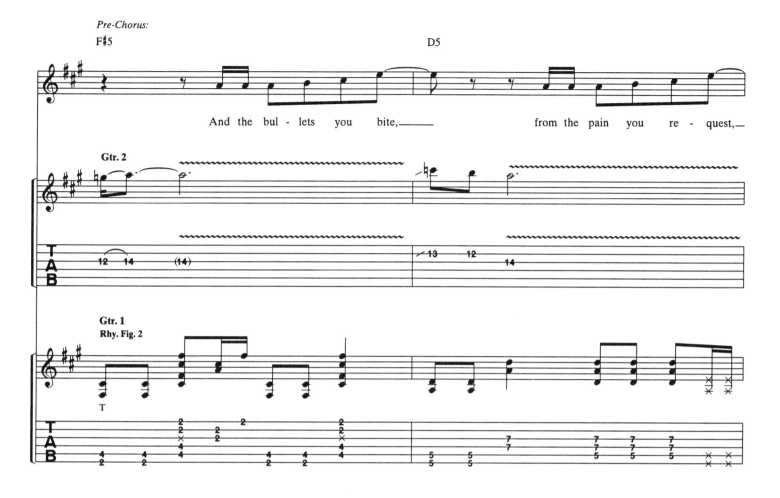

And the bul - lets you bite,_____ from the pain you re - quest,_

_____ you're find - ing them hard - er to_____ di - gest._

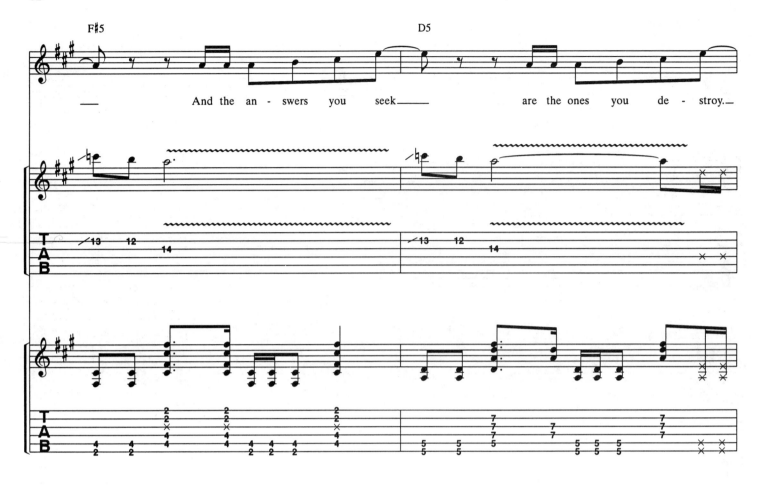

And the an-swers you seek____ are the ones you de-stroy.____

Your an-ger's well de - ployed.

end Rhy. Fig. 2

Verse 2:
Hey, you now hunger, feeding your mind with selfishness.
Hey, you now wander aimlessly around your consciousness.
When your prophecies fail and your thoughts become weak,
Silence creates necessity.
You're clothing yourself in the shields of despair,
Your courage now impaired.
(To Chorus:)

MAYBE

Words and Music by
ED ROLAND

16

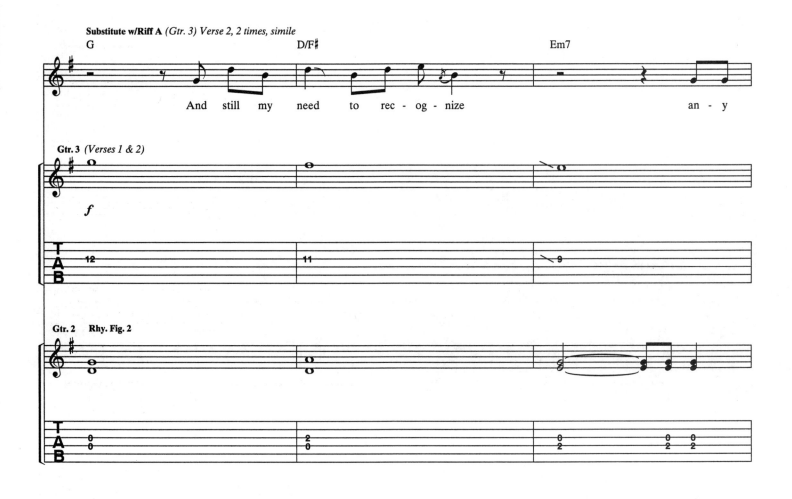

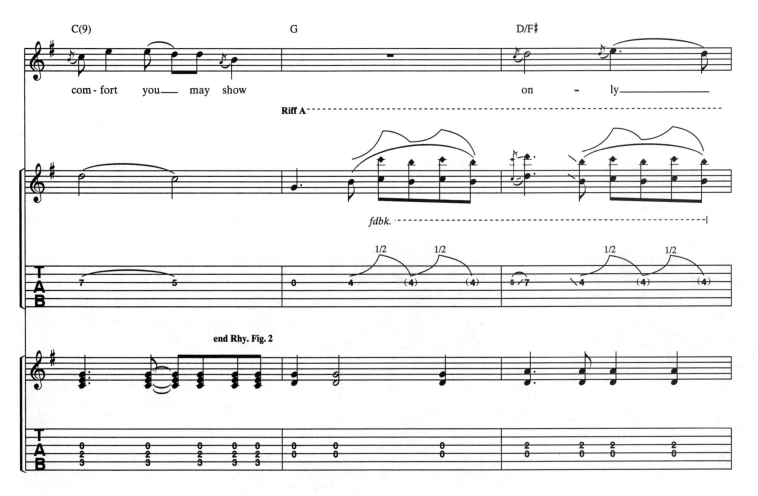

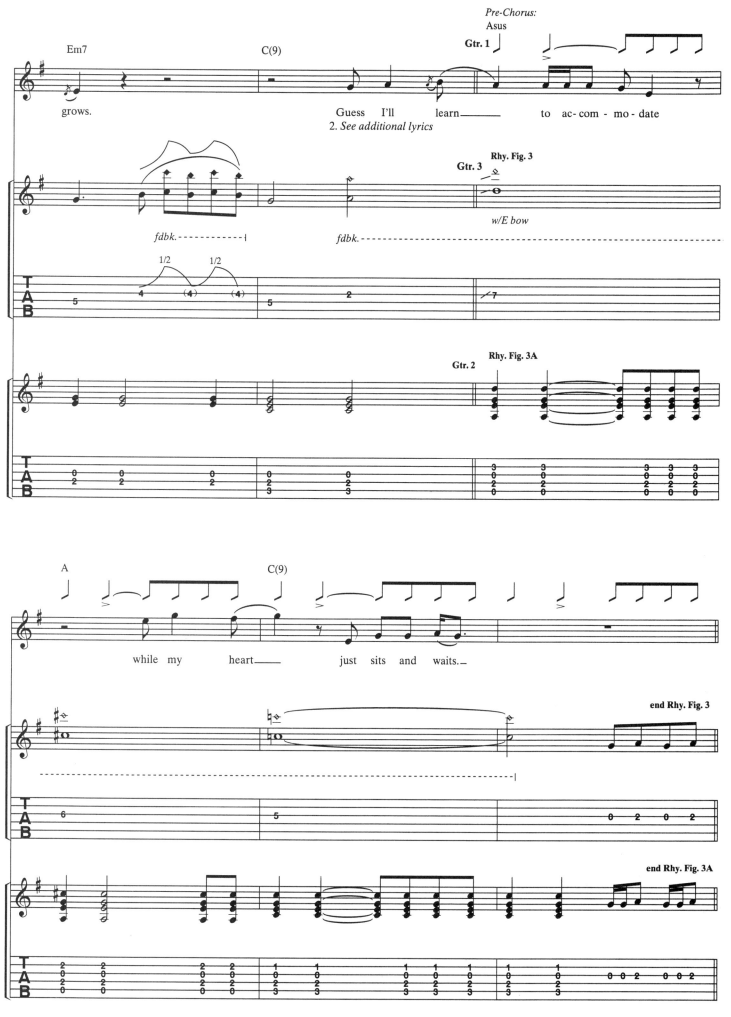

20

Interlude:
w/Rhy. Figs. 1 (Gtr. 1) & 1A (Gtr. 2) 2 times, simile

Guitar Solo:
w/Rhy. Figs. 1 (Gtr. 1) & 2 (Gtr. 2) 2 times, simile

May - be____ God you found. May - be____

____ is all that you____ can of - fer now, of - fer

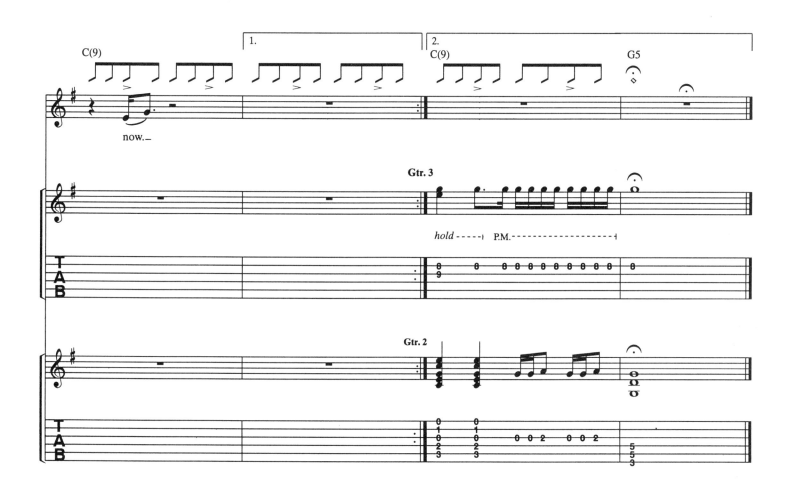

now.____

Verse 2:
Where am I to take refuge
When the storms of pain release?
Shelter me.
This blessedness of life
Sometimes brings me to my knees.
I call on thee.
(To Pre-Chorus 2:)

Pre-Chorus 2:
I have not the words to write
A farewell to you tonight.
(To Chorus:)

FULL CIRCLE

Words and Music by
ED ROLAND

One fine morning I'll a-wake to sleep some

more. 2. De

fine my pre-mo-ni-tions, last judge-ment and con-di-tions. I'd have to

3. See additional lyrics

dig in my e-mo-tions, but then re-lin-quish my de-vo-tion.

One fine morning I'll a-wake, then hope to

learn.

One fine morning I'll a-wake to love's re-

Full Circle - 7 - 2
0028B

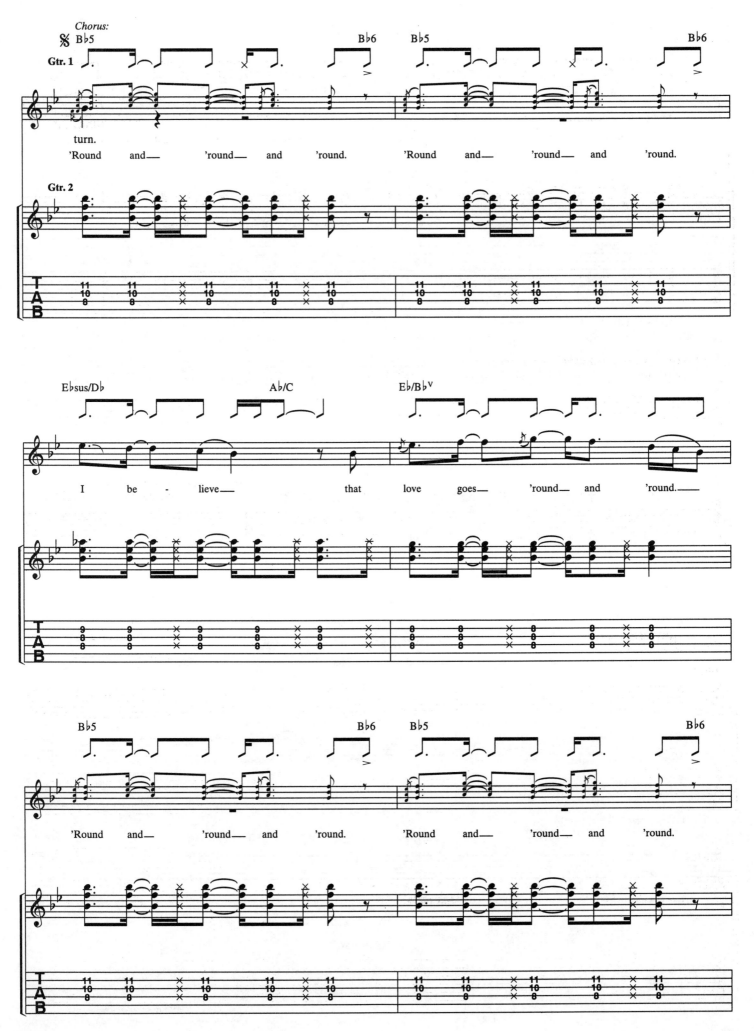

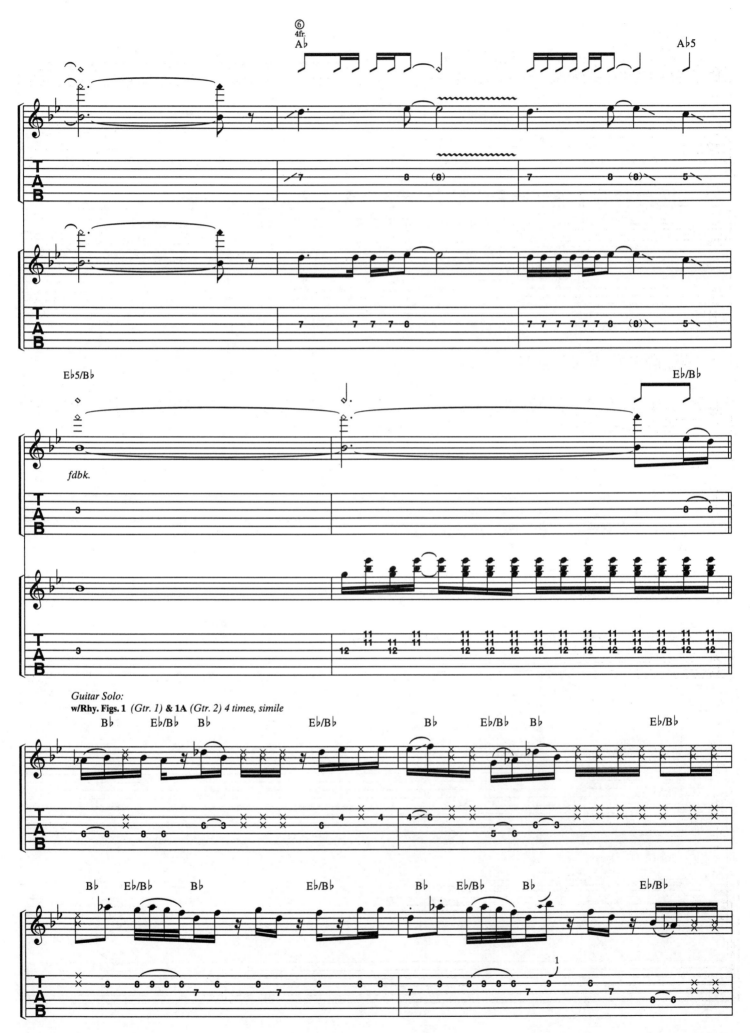

*Chords based on overall tonality throughout section.

Verse 3:
Singing the rendition of hope in my condition.
Caught up in defending that truth is never-ending.
One fine morning I'll awake, then reaffirm.
One fine morning I'll awake to love's return.
(To Chorus:)

BLAME

Words and Music by
ED ROLAND

Gtr. 1 is tuned to "open D" and Capo III:
⑥=D ③=F♯
⑤=A ②=A
④=D ①=D

Tempo I (Slowly ♩ = 74)
Intro:

*Capo III, sounding key is F.

32

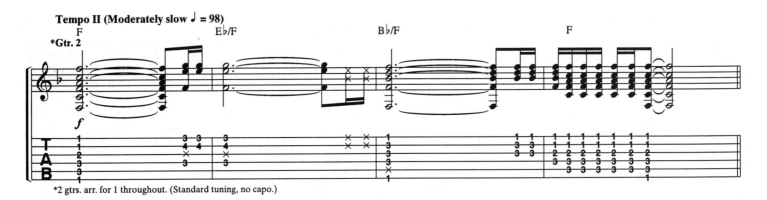

*2 gtrs. arr. for 1 throughout. (Standard tuning, no capo.)

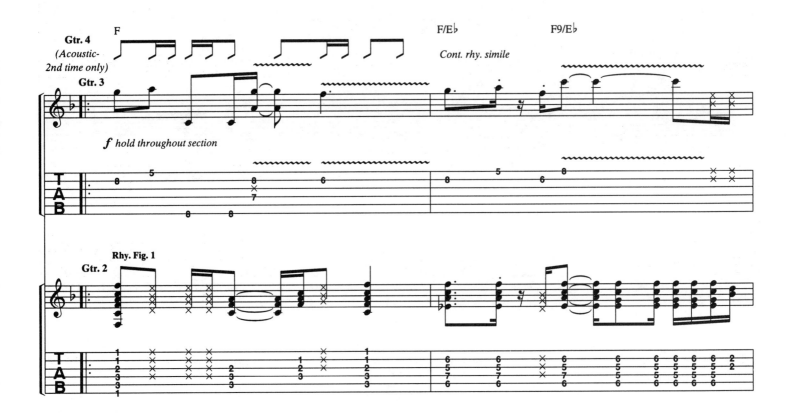

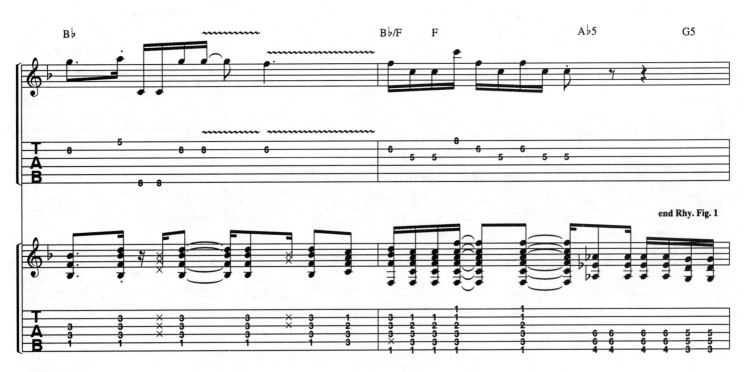

34

Verse 2:
You lay me out
In hopes that I'd wilt away.
But strength rained down
And love provided shade.
(To Pre-Chorus 2:)

Pre-Chorus 2:
So while the pageant of lies
Still glows from your tongue,
Don't blame me for your Kingdom Come.
(To Chorus:)

DISCIPLINED BREAKDOWN

Words and Music by
ED ROLAND

42

Wel - come, all,————— to my dis - ci - plined— break -

down. Break - down, break - down, break - down.

Verse 2:
I never, ever can decipher who listens to the words I say.
While I sense I'm searching, I never know who's lurking
To scare my sacred thoughts away.
I'd love to hang and chat awhile,
But my mind's become vile.
(To Chorus:)

Verse 3:
I never, ever can contribute to finding all the faults that sustain,
Never mind the answers to who spreads the cancer,
When the questioning of why remains.
I'd love to sit and rationalize, but my tongue's become dry.
(To Chorus:)

Disciplined Breakdown - 5 - 5
0028B

FORGIVENESS

Words and Music by
ED ROLAND

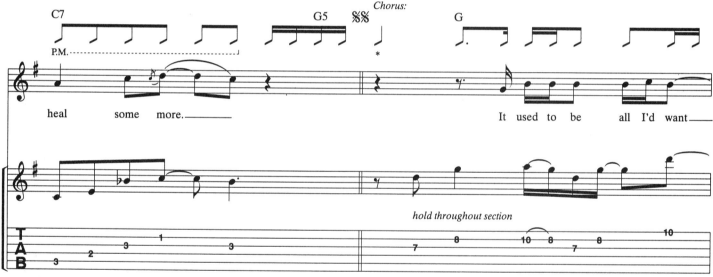

*Electric & Acoustic gtrs. arr. for 1.

Forgiveness - 8 - 2
0028B

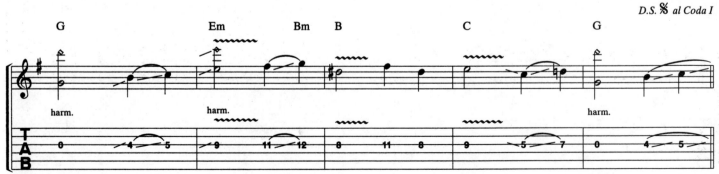

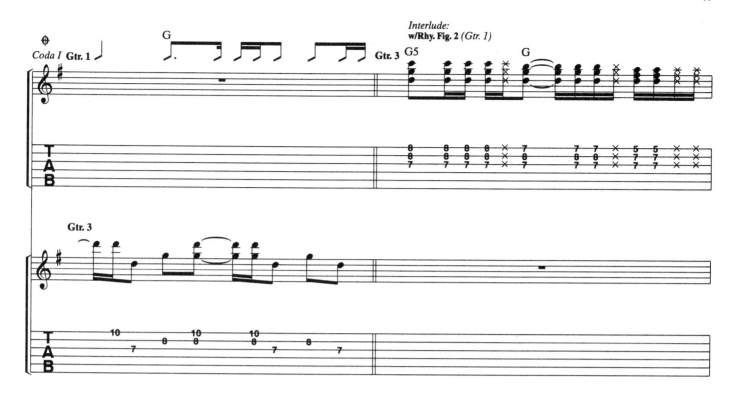

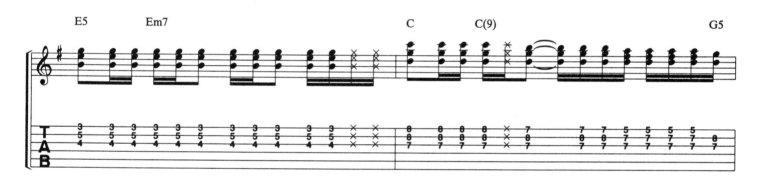

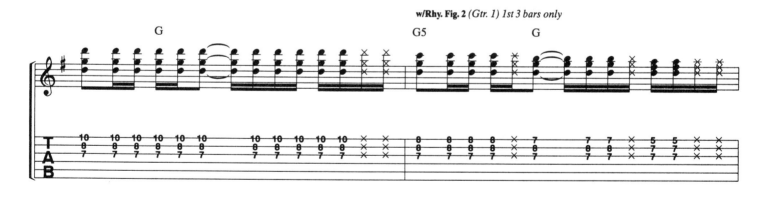

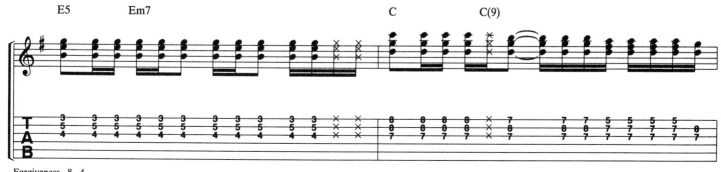

Forgiveness - 8 - 4
0028B

48

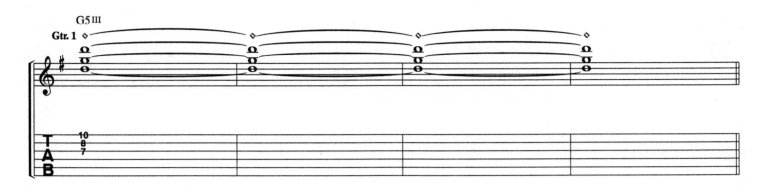

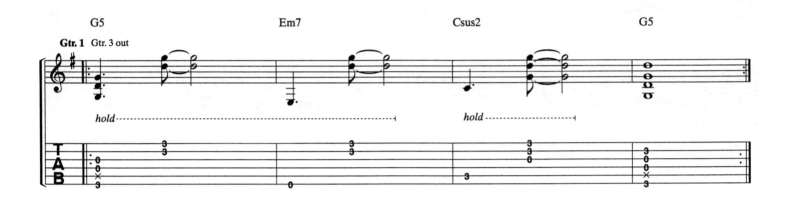

w/Rhy. Fig. 2 *(Gtr. 1) 2 times, simile*

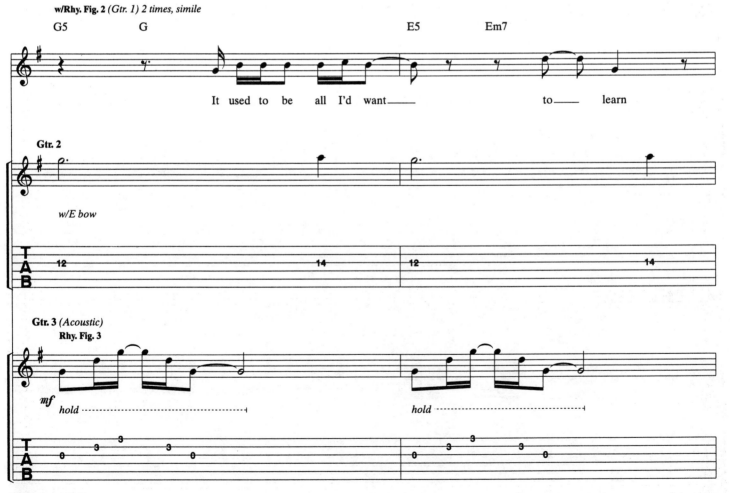

It used to be all I'd want____ to____ learn

was wis - dom, trust___ and truth.___

end Rhy. Fig. 3

hold

hold

Now___ all I real - ly want_____ to_____ learn

D.S. 𝄋𝄋 al Coda II

is for - give - ness___ for you.

harm.

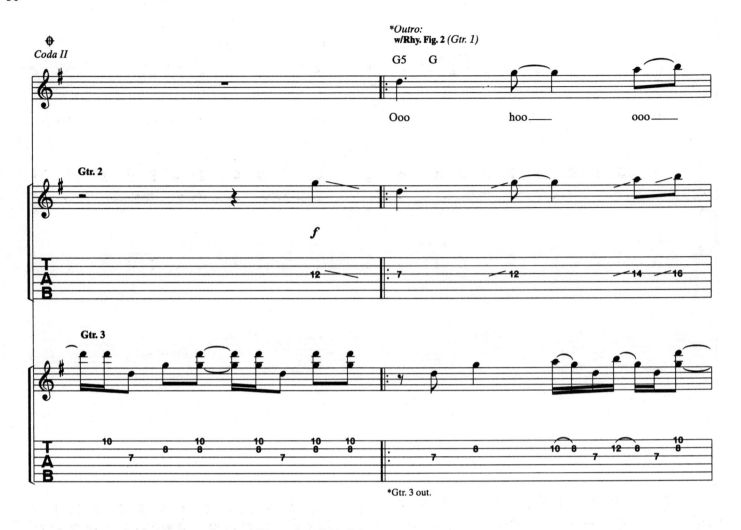

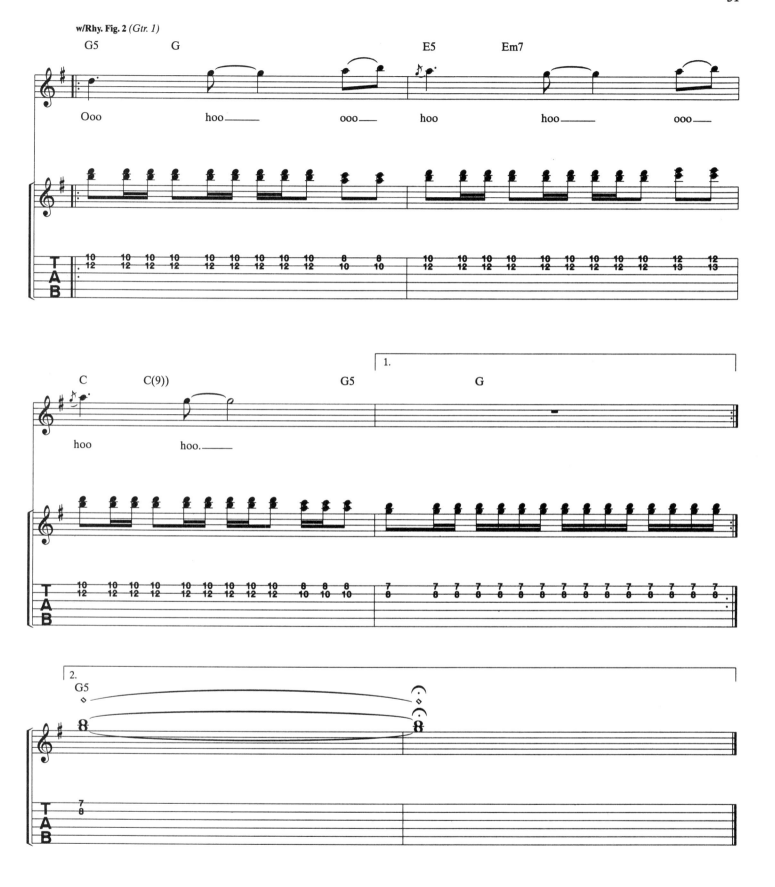

Verse 2:
As my seasons change, I've now grown to know
When one's heart creates, one's soul doesn't owe.
So I wash away the stains of yesterday,
Then tempt my heart with loves display.
(To Chorus:)

LINK

Words and Music by
ED ROLAND

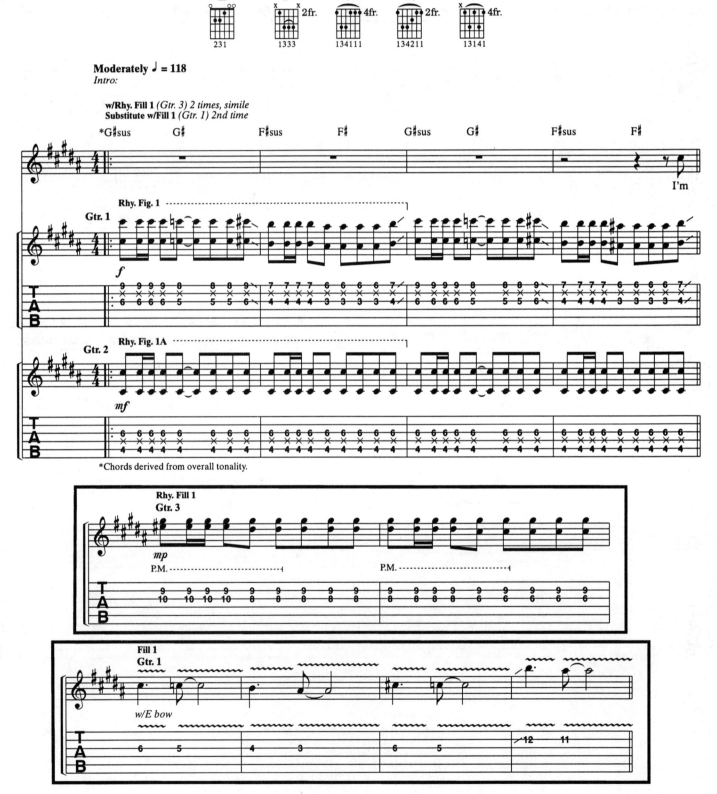

*Chords derived from overall tonality.

Verse 2:
I'm sleeping, sleeping to develop myself.
I wake up, wake up then relinquish what's left.
(To Chorus:)

GIVING

Words and Music by
ED ROLAND

Verse 2:
You're giving me calm to fall into,
Giving me hope to guide me through,
And I want more, I want more.
Giving me light to see through tears,
Giving me strength to crash my fears,
And I want more, I want more.
Still, all I need is love,
So give me more.
(To Chorus:)

Verse 3:
You're giving me choice so I may seek,
Giving me faith so I'll believe,
And I want more, I want more.
Giving me breath of your mercy,
Giving yourself to comfort me,
And I want more, I want more.
Still, all I need is love,
So give me more.
(To Outro:)

IN BETWEEN

Words and Music by
ED ROLAND

In Between - 7 - 1
0028B

*Chord symbols reflect combinad tonality.

64

And the si - lence fills— the void— of love and hate;

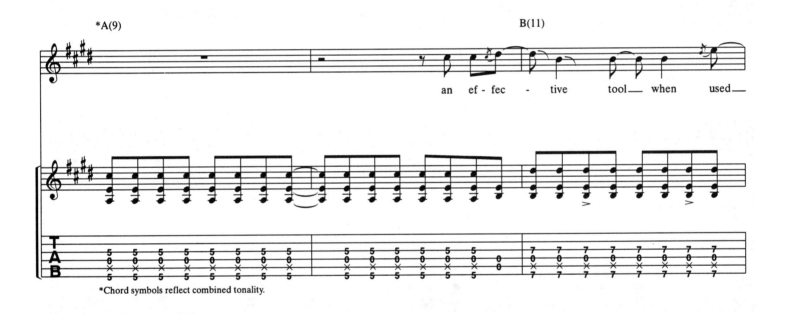

an ef - fec - tive tool— when used—

*Chord symbols reflect combined tonality.

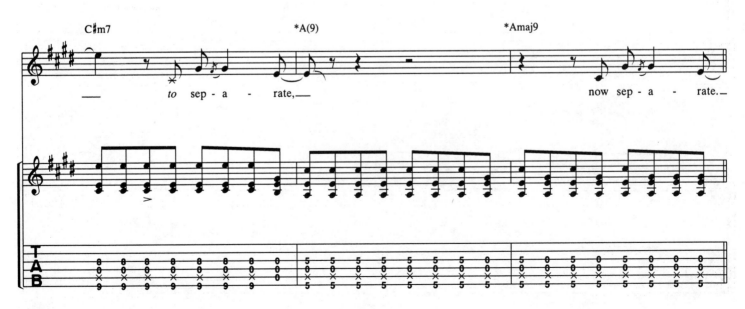

— to sep - a - rate,— now sep - a - rate.

Verse 3:
In between us,
Hope we've yet to see.
We long for healings,
But the scars, they never leave.
(To Chorus:)

CROWDED HEAD

Words and Music by
ED ROLAND

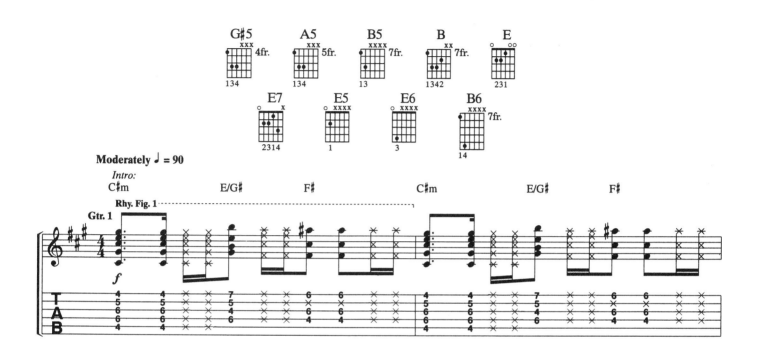

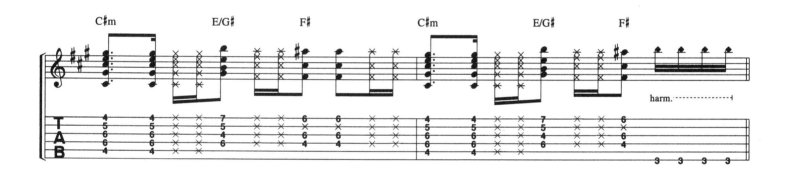

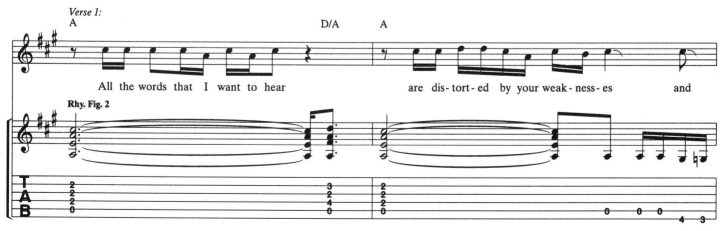

Crowded Head - 7 - 1
0028B

68

Crowded Head - 7 - 2
0028B

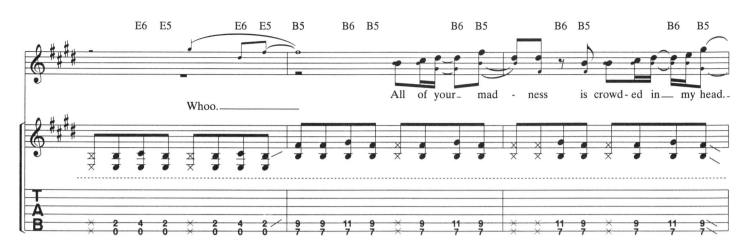

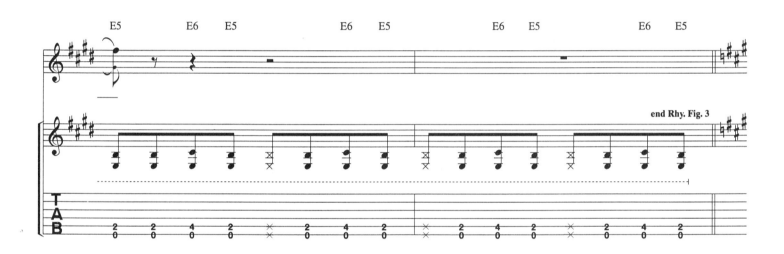

Verse 2:
w/Rhy. Fig. 2 *(Gtr. 1)*

And the peace that I real-ly need, you sub-sti-tute it for your pol-i-cy___ of

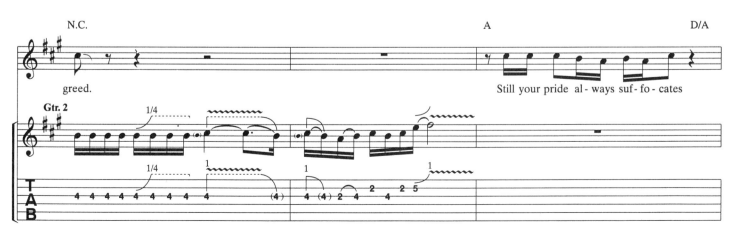

greed. Still your pride al-ways suf-fo-cates

Crowded Head - 7 - 3
0028B

Chorus:
w/Rhy. Fig. 3 *(Gtr. 1)*

All of your sad - ness is crowd - ed in my head.

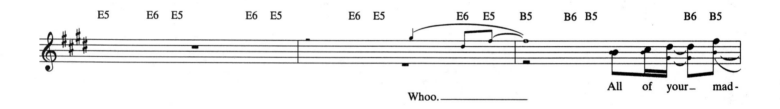

Whoo. All of your mad -

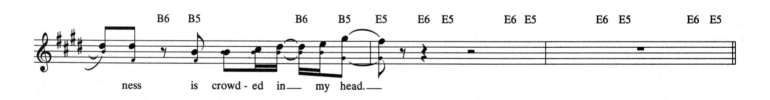

ness is crowd - ed in my head.

Bridge:
G#5

With all your stat - ic, I can't dis - tin - guish be - tween what's be - ing said.

w/delay throughout section

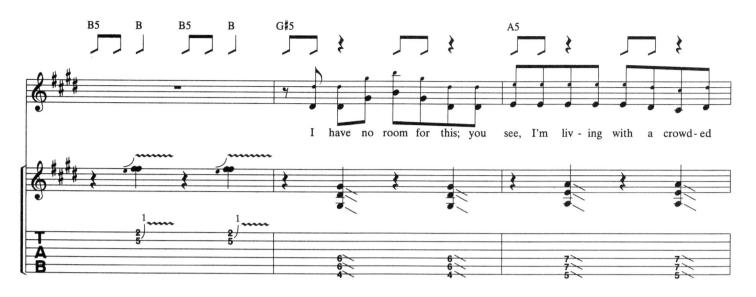

I have no room for this; you see, I'm liv-ing with a crowd-ed

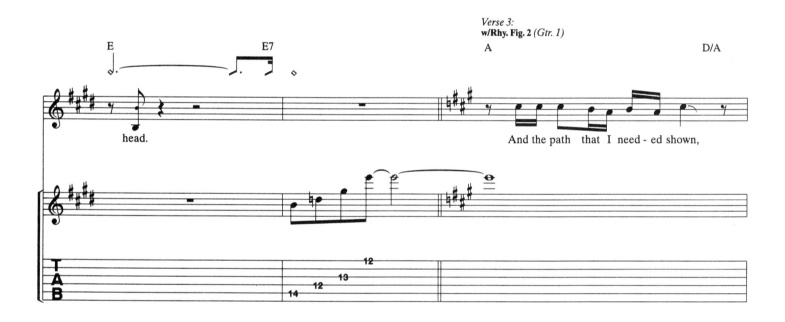

head.

And the path that I need-ed shown,

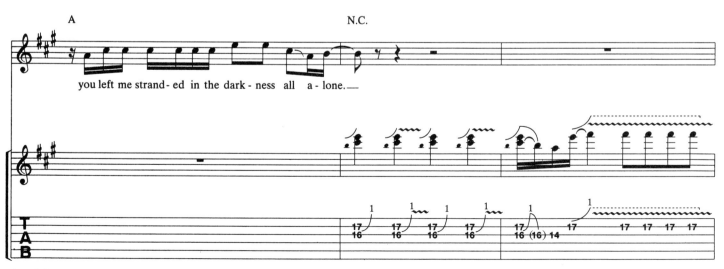

you left me strand-ed in the dark-ness all a-lone.

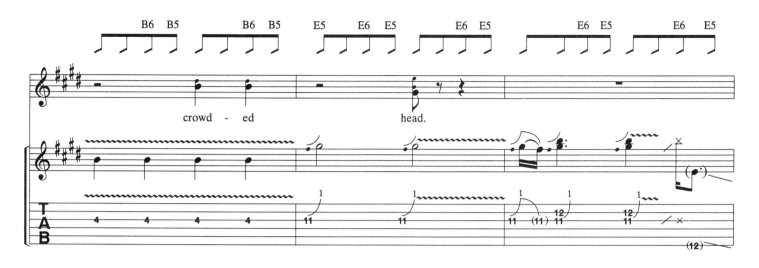

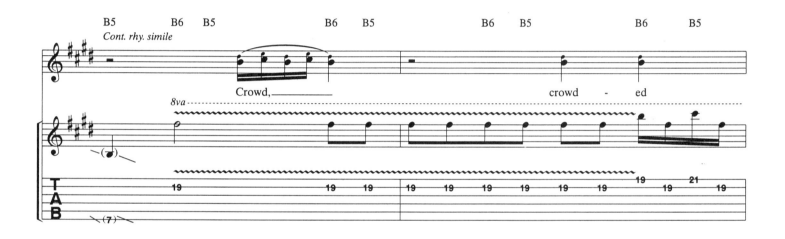

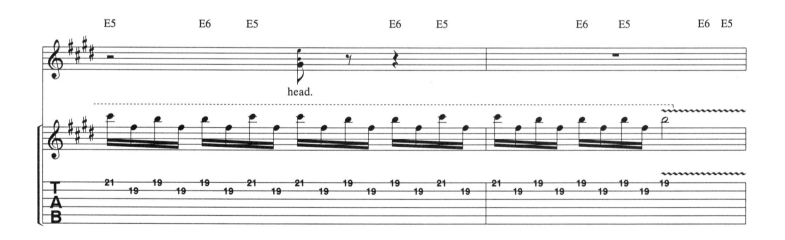

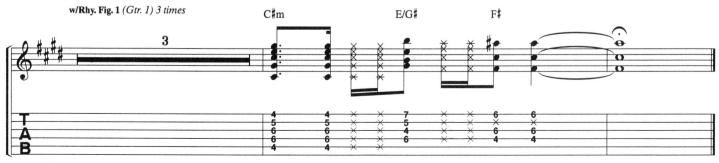

Crowded Head - 7 - 7
0028B

EVERYTHING

Words and Music by
ED ROLAND

All gtrs. tune down 1/2 step:
⑥=E♭ ③=G♭
⑤=A♭ ②=B♭
④=D♭ ①=E♭

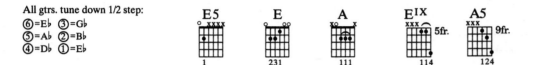

Moderately ♩ = 136

Intro:

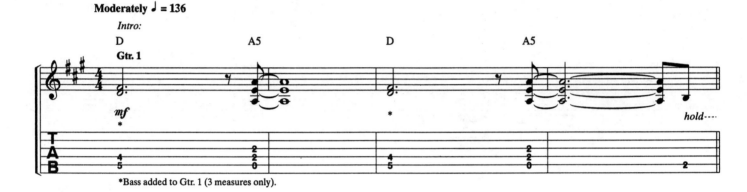

*Bass added to Gtr. 1 (3 measures only).

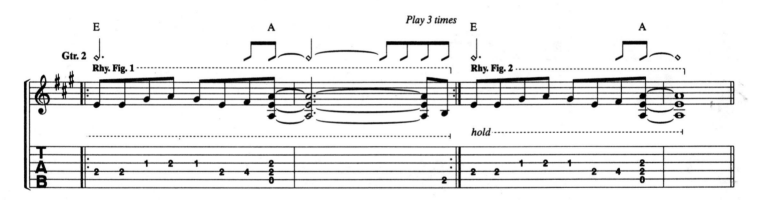

Verse:

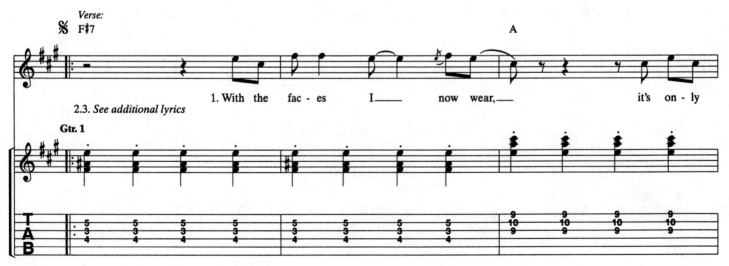

1. With the fac-es I___ now wear,___ it's on-ly

2.3. *See additional lyrics*

Everything - 4 - 1
0028B

Everything - 4 - 2
0028B

Verse 2:
And this comfort I've designed
Will only stay intact until the truth I find.
As some answer fly around, no cure have I found.
(To Chorus:)

Verse 3:
The reflection I now see is always
Trying to blind and discourage me.
But my patience shall prevail,
And myself as well.
(To Chorus:)

GUITAR TAB GLOSSARY **

TABLATURE EXPLANATION

READING TABLATURE: Tablature illustrates the six strings of the guitar. Notes and chords are indicated by the placement of fret numbers on a given string(s).

String ⑥, 3rd Fret String ① 12th Fret A "C" Chord C Chord Arpeggiated
String ③ 13th Fret

BENDING NOTES

HALF STEP: Play the note and bend string one half step.*

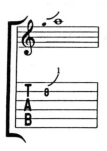

WHOLE STEP: Play the note and bend string one whole step.

WHOLE STEP AND A HALF: Play the note and bend string a whole step and a half.

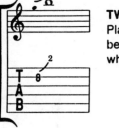

TWO STEPS: Play the note and bend string two whole steps.

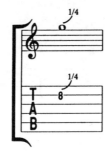

SLIGHT BEND (Microtone): Play the note and bend string slightly to the equivalent of half a fret.

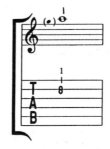

PREBEND (Ghost Bend): Bend to the specified note, before the string is picked.

PREBEND AND RELEASE: Bend the string, play it, then release to the original note.

REVERSE BEND: Play the already-bent string, then immediately drop it down to the fretted note.

BEND AND RELEASE: Play the note and gradually bend to the next pitch, then release to the original note. Only the first note is attacked.

BENDS INVOLVING MORE THAN ONE STRING: Play the note and bend string while playing an additional note (or notes) on another string(s). Upon release, relieve pressure from additional note(s), causing original note to sound alone.

BENDS INVOLVING STATIONARY NOTES: Play notes and bend lower pitch, then hold until release begins (indicated at the point where line becomes solid).

UNISON BEND: Play both notes and immediately bend the lower note to the same pitch as the higher note.

DOUBLE NOTE BEND: Play both notes and immediately bend both strings simultaneously.

*A half step is the smallest interval in Western music; it is equal to one fret. A whole step equals two frets.

© 1990 Beam Me Up Music
c/o CPP/Belwin, Inc. Miami, Florida 33014
International Copyright Secured   Made in U.S.A.   All Rights Reserved   **By Kenn Chipkin and Aaron Stang